Cover illustration by Richard Johnson
Text and illustrations copyright © the individual illustrators and authors 2019
The Migrations Project was initiated by Andy Robert Davies, Stephen Fowler, Piet Grobler, Tobias Hickey
and Becky Palmer of the International Centre for the Picture Book in Society, University of Worcester

I|C|P|B|S INTERNATIONAL CENTRE FOR THE PICTURE BOOK IN SOCIETY

First published in Great Britain in 2019 by Otter-Barry Books,
Little Orchard, Burley Gate, Herefordshire, HR1 3QS
www.otterbarrybooks.com

All rights reserved

ISBN 978-1-91095-980-0

Printed in China
3 5 7 9 8 6 4 2

FSC
www.fsc.org

MIX
Paper from
responsible sources
FSC® C104723

MIGRATIONS
Open Hearts Open Borders

Edited by The International Centre for the Picture Book in Society

Otter-Barry BOOKS

Contents

The images presented here are a selection from the hundreds sent in by children's book illustrators across the world, for an exhibition entitled *Migrations*. Its aim is to express support for and solidarity with the hundreds of thousands of human migrants who face immense difficulties and dangers in their struggle to find a better and safer place to live.

Shaun Tan writes:

All migration is an act of imagination, a flight of imagination. A hope that frequently exercises a previously unknown human potential. Migration is also an act of imagination that all too often ends in despair, from death at sea and psychological trauma due to the intolerance of host communities, ignorant hostility, poverty and illness. What can be done? The universe of stars looks down but does not even ask this question. That's for us, the living, the thinking and feeling: descendants through millennia of successful migration – whose ancestors dreamed of something better as they fled across deserts and oceans and ice bridges. It's left for us to imagine what to do, to pass on the dividends of hope that have been invested in us.

Can small gestures – a picture, a friendly message – make a difference? By creating, looking, asking questions, confronting despair, we invest back into an economy far greater than any stock exchange, far nobler than any political system. We help sustain the will to imagine a better world, for adults and especially children, for whom the positive inspiration of art and story can never be overestimated. Like the Arctic Tern, setting out for a new nest some 20,000 km away, flying through darkness with only the thinnest of magnetic songs for bearings, the migrant moves into the unknown, which holds both promises and fears. Should the imagination of some falter and weaken, whether that of the migrant or the host community, then it must help to look upon the thousands of other shapes just beyond our wingtips, flying in vast formation, and know that we will never be alone.

Migrations, an exhibition of the International Centre for the Picture Book in Society, was first shown at BIBIANA, Bratislava, in September 2017. The ICPBS, founded at the University of Worcester, England, by Piet Grobler and Tobias Hickey, emphasises and celebrates the power of illustration to engage with society, particularly by focusing on issues of cultural diversity and the inclusivity of minorities and socially disenfranchised people.

Passenger Pigeon

Diek Grobler – South Africa

Departures

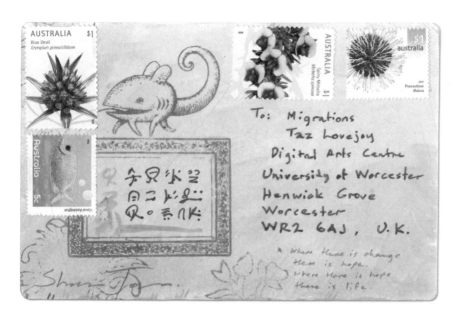

Where there is change
there is hope.

Where there is hope
there is life.

Shaun Tan – Australia

DIGITAL ARTS CENTRE
UNIVERSITY OF
WORCESTER
HENWICK GROVE
WORCESTER
UK   WR2 6AJ

Jon Klassen – Canada/USA

A migração mais comum nas aves é a fuga sazonal ao inverno, ao frio e à falta de alimento. É talvez a melhor metáfora para o movimento migratório dos refugiados: outra fuga, e não um abandono permanente. Que tal como os pássaros, os migrantes encontrem a primavera onde quer que cheguem. E também nos lugares de onde partiram, se quiserem voltar.

To:
MiGRATioNS exhibition
(iCPBS illustration)
Digital Arts Centre
University of Worcester
Henwick Grove
Worcester
WR2 6AJ
United Kingdom

Birds migrate in a seasonal escape from winter, with its cold and lack of food. And perhaps a better way to see the migration of refugees is as another escape, not a permanent departure. Like the birds, the migrants find Spring wherever they come. And [hopefully] also in the place they left, if they should ever wish to return.

Catarina Sobral – Portugal

In the end
we only regret
the chances we
didn't take.
It begins with
a single step...

Royal Mail
14-06-2017

Premier
Mail Centre

MIGRATIONS EXHIBITION
TAZ LOVEJOY
DIGITAL ARTS CENTRE
UNIVERSITY OF WORCESTER
HENWICK GROVE
WORCESTER
WR2 6AJ

Rhian Wyn Harrison 2017

In the end we only regret the chances we didn't take.
It begins with a single step...

Rhian Wyn Harrison – UK

Fly and flow.

Alessandra Cimatoribus – Italy

"BEYOND THE CLOUDS"

RAIN AND MOUNTAINS

Don't forget
Father's Day
Sunday 18 June

Royal Mail Mount Pleasant
Mail Centre
Birmingham
Mail Centre
.06.17
03.00 am
50600425

YUVAL ZOMMER

MIGRATIONS exhibition
Taz Lovejoy
Digital Arts Centre
University of Worcester
Henwick Grove
WORCESTER UK
WR2 6AJ

Beyond the clouds, rain and mountains...

Yuval Zommer – UK

Katerina Dubovik
адрас адпраўшчыка і Індэкс прадпрыемства сувязі

Катерина Дубовик
Купцувщина
220017, Минк

ПРЫЯРЫТЭТНАЕ
PRIORITAIRE

R RR520521375BY

RECOMMANDE

Migrations exhibition
Каму *Taz Lovejoy, Digital Arts*
Centre, University of Worcester
Куды *Henwik Grove*
Worcester WR2 6AJ
Індэкс *United*
Kingdom
Великобритание

24

Katerina Dubovik – Belarus

Everything is possible.
You were born free.

27   Petr Horáček – Czech Republic/UK

Kana Okita – Japan

28

Hope!

Long Journeys

As free from danger as the heavens are free
From pain and toil, there would they build and be,
And sail about the world to scenes unheard
Of and unseen – O, were they but a bird!

John Clare

31
Becky Palmer – UK

27 June 2017

THE SKIES HAVE
No BORDERS.

From christopher corr

MIGRATIONS exhibition
TAZ LoveJoY
DIGITAL ARTS CENTRE
University of Worcester
Henwick Grove
Worcester
WR2 6AJ

The skies have no borders.

33   Christopher Corr – UK

We are all travellers in the wilderness of this world, and the best we can find in our travels is an honest friend.
Robert Louis Stevenson

35　　　Andy Robert Davies – UK

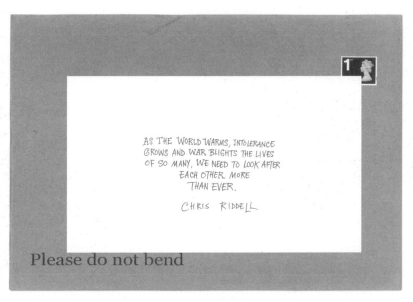

AS THE WORLD WARMS, INTOLERANCE
GROWS AND WAR BLIGHTS THE LIVES
OF SO MANY, WE NEED TO LOOK AFTER
EACH OTHER MORE
THAN EVER.

CHRIS RIDDELL

Please do not bend

As the world warms, intolerance
grows and war blights the lives
of so many, we need to look after
each other more
than ever.

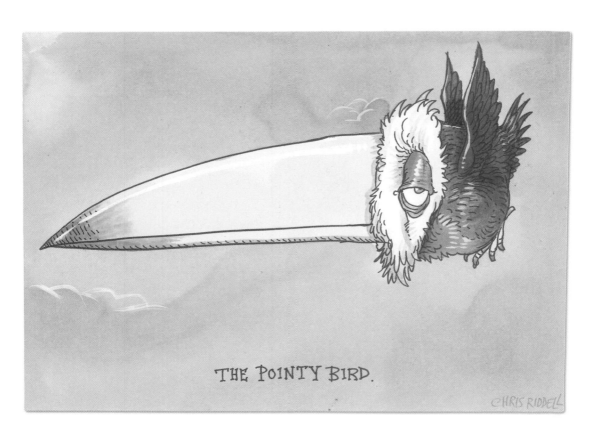

THE POINTY BIRD.

CHRIS RIDDELL

37

Chris Riddell – UK

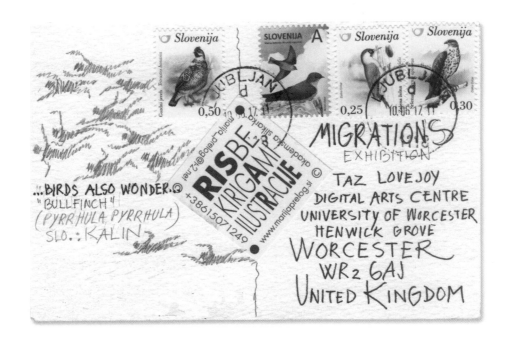

...BIRDS ALSO WONDER. ©
"BULLFINCH"
(PYRRHULA PYRRHULA)
SLO.: KALIN

MIGRATIONS
EXHIBITION

TAZ LOVEJOY
DIGITAL ARTS CENTRE
UNIVERSITY OF WORCESTER
HENWICK GROVE
WORCESTER
WR2 6AJ
UNITED KINGDOM

Birds also wonder...

39

Marija Prelog – Slovenia

No importa de donde
vengas, ni tus colores
a donde llegues, siempre
existirá alguien de
buen corazón dispuesto
a ayudarte.
Sólo ten un buen viaje!

———

Patricia González Palacios
Santiago - Chile

MG:
Exhibition
Taz Lovejoy
Digital Arts Centre
University of Worcester
Henwick Grove
Worcester
WR2 GAJ

United Kingdom

No matter where you come from, what colour you are,
or where you come to, there will always be someone
of good heart to help you.
Only travel safely!

Patricia Gonzalez Palacios – Chile

I think we are finally going somewhere safe...

Leila Ajiri – Germany

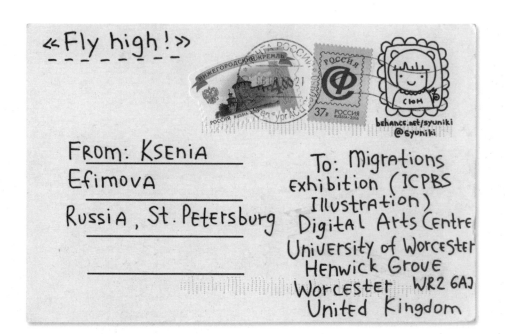

«Fly high!»

FROM: KSENIA
Efimova
RussiA, St. Petersburg

To: Migrations
exhibition (ICPBS
Illustration)
Digital Arts Centre
University of Worcester
Henwick Grove
Worcester WR2 6AJ
United Kingdom

behance.net/syuniki
@syuniki

Fly high!

Ksenia Efimova – Russia

BIRDS FLY

Some with one leg
Some with one eye
Some with one heart

MIGRATIONS exhibition
Taz Lovejoy
Digital Arts Centre
University of Worcester
Henwick Grove
Worcester
WR2 6AJ

Jungtine Karalystė

PIRMENYBINĖ
PRIORITAIRE

ROMB-BOMB.COM
FACEBOOK.COM/
ILLUSTRATEDTEXTILE

Birds fly
Some with one leg
Some with one eye
Some with one heart

47

'FLY BY NIGHT'
by Neal Layton
for the
MIGRATIONS
EXHIBITION
pencil, ink and collage digitally
combined with some hand colouring

TO
TA2 LOVEJOY
DIGITAL ARTS CENTRE
UNIVERSITY OF WORCESTER
HENWICK GROVE
WORCESTER
WR2 6AJ
U.K.

Royal Mail
06.05.17

Southampton, Portsmouth & IOW

'Fly by Night'

Neal Layton – UK

Saviour says: Be nice.
(What's so difficult about that?)

Inga Grimm – Sweden

I fly alone during the night looking for a place to carry on my life.
The swallow

Travel well!

María León – Spain

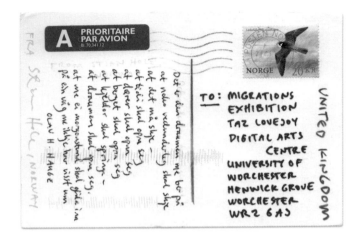

It's that dream that we carry with us
that something wonderful will happen,
that it has to happen,
that time will open,
that the heart will open,
that doors will open,
that the mountains will open,
that wells will leap up,
that the dream will open,
that one morning we'll slip in
to a harbor that we've never known.

Det er den Draumen by Olav H. Hauge,
translated by Robert Bly

Stian Hole – Norway

POST CARD

From: Satoko Watanabe

To: MIGRATIONS exhibition
(ICPBS Illustration)
Digital Arts Center
University of Worcester
Henwick Grove
Worcester WR 2 6 A J

United Kingdom

VIA AIR MAIL

A little bird flies in the sky.
A little bird is damaged.
A little bird needs a place to take a rest.

A little bird flies in the sky.
A little bird is damaged.
A little bird needs a place to take a rest.

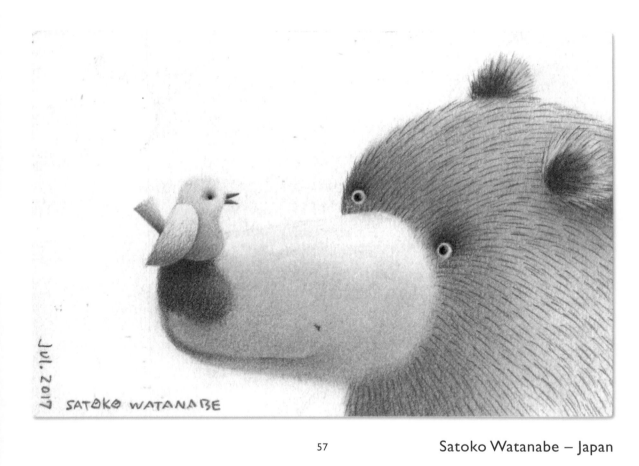

Jul. 2017

SATOKO WATANABE

57

Satoko Watanabe – Japan

The albatross holds in its eye, the
storm
And, over more miles than lie between
us and the moon,
The small green island of its home.

Taz Lovejoy

Words and picture come with
love from
Nicola Davies
Wales

Digital Arts Centre
University of Worcester
Henwick Grove
Worcester
WR 2 6 AJ

www. nicola-davies. com

The albatross holds in its eye the storm
And, over more miles than lie between us and the moon,
The small green island of its home.

Nicola Davies – UK

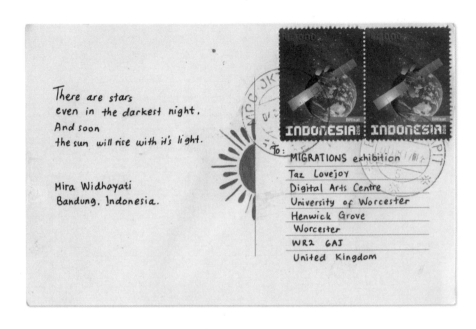

There are stars
even in the darkest night,
And soon
the sun will rise with it's light.

Mira Widhayati
Bandung, Indonesia.

To:
MIGRATIONS exhibition
Taz Lovejoy
Digital Arts Centre
University of Worcester
Henwick Grove
Worcester
WR2 6AJ
United Kingdom

There are stars
even in the darkest night.
And soon
the sun will rise with its light.

Mira Widhayati – Indonesia

Axel Scheffler – UK

Borders – not what they used to be

Arrivals

From up here I see no borders.

65   Natalia Gurovich – Chile/Mexico

Your everyday is their childhood.

Judith Drews – Germany

One can always go and one can always return.

SIEMPRE PODER IR
SIEMPRE PODER VOLVER

69   Gabriela Germain Fonck – Chile

To.

Piet Grobler C/o Mr Marian Potrok
MIGRATIONS- project
International Center for the Picture Book in Society
c/o BIBIANA, Medzinárodný dom umenia pre deti
Panská ul. 41,
815 39 Bratislava
Slovakia

Open the door.

Myungae Lee – Korea

My dream for everyone all around the globe is to have a legendary bird that can fly to wherever that they love to travel, without fear.

Having a good life is everyone's right. So try to make these wishes become reality.

Mohammad Barrangi Fashtami – Iran

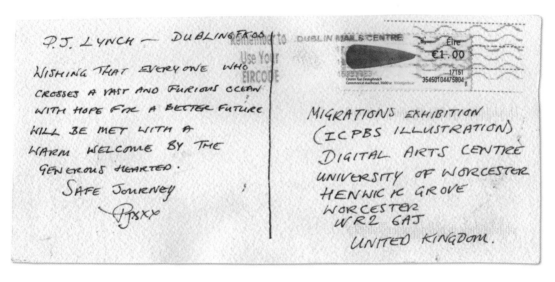

Wishing that everyone who crosses a vast
and furious ocean with hope for a better future
will be met with a warm welcome by the generous hearted.
Safe journey.

PJ Lynch – Ireland

May 31st 2017
Imagination
and knowledge,
words and ideas
fly over fences,
barbed wire,
brick walls, through
prison bars, stormy
skies and borders...

Marie-Louise Gay (Canada)

MIGRATIONS Exhibition
Digital Arts Centre
University of Worcester
Henwick Grove
Worcester
WR2 6AJ
United Kingdom

STELLA Canada

STELLA Canada

STELLA Canada

17·05·12·112
3878 H4T

Imagination and knowledge, words and ideas
fly over fences, barbed wire, brick walls,
through prison bars, stormy skies and borders...

76

Marie-Louise Gay – Canada

NEW FRIENDS
COMING
FROM AFAR
BRING US
DIFFERENT
TALES!

MARCELO PIMENTEL

RIO DE JANEIRO · BRAZIL

MIGRATIONS
EXHIBITION
Taz Lovejoy
Digital Arts Center
University of Worcester
Henwick Grove
WR2·6AJ Worcester
UNITED KINGDOM – UK

New friends coming from afar
bring us different tales!

Marcelo Pimentel – Brazil

'PRIORITY'

81   Helena Bergendahl – Sweden

There are no strangers here;
Only friends you haven't yet met.

Ascribed to William Butler Yeats.

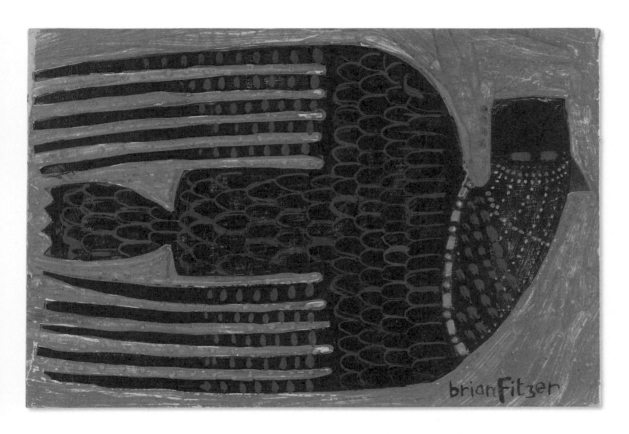

Brian Fitzer – Ireland

All the Children of the World Should feel Safe and Cherished

Mies van Hout

Hope for the Future

godspeed.

I wish you
well upon your
way.

To: Migrations exhibition
D. A. C. Illustration
UNIVERSITY OF WORCESTER
HENWICK Grove
WORCESTER
WR2 6 AJ
United Kingdom

FROM PIET GROBLER

Godspeed.
I wish you well upon your way.

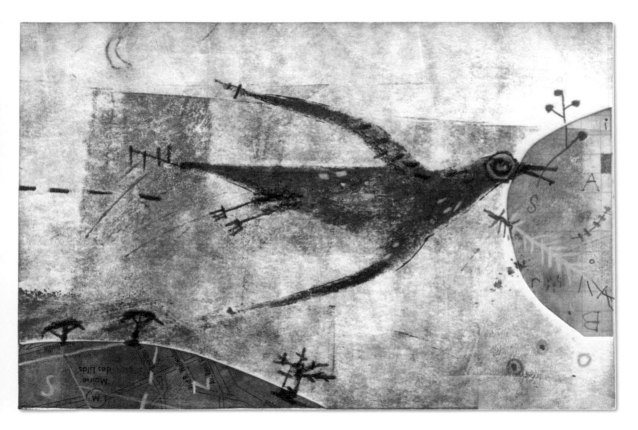

Piet Grobler – South Africa

We are one!

Nelleke Verhoeff – Netherlands

THE SPAN
OF THE EARTH
IS OUR
LIMTLESS
EXPANSION
ROGER MELLO

ADDRESS
to:
PIET GROBLER
c/o Mr. MARIAN POTROK
MIGRATIONS-PROJECT
INTERNATIONAL CENTER FOR
THE PICTURE BOOK IN SOCIETY
c/o BIBIANA
MEDZINÁRODNÝ DOM
UMENIA PRE DETI
PANSKÁ UL. 41,
815 39 BRATISLAVA
SLOVAKIA

The span of the Earth is our limitless expansion.

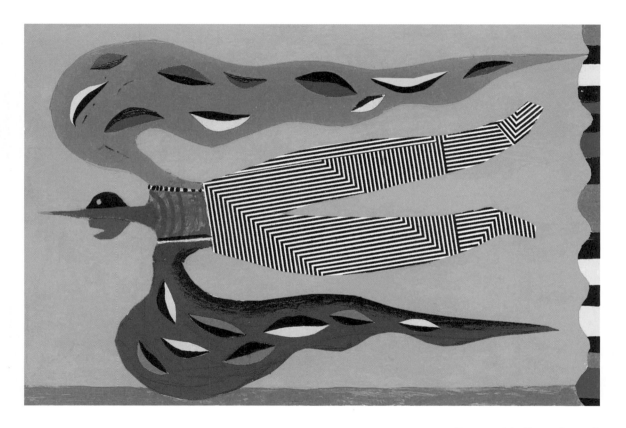

91

Roger Mello – Brazil

COMPARTIR
EL MUNDO
EN PAZ Y
LIBERTAD.
LA TIERRA
Y LAS PERSONAS
NO TIENEN
DUEÑO.

ISOL

MIGRATIONS
exhibition
Taz Lovejoy
Digital Arts Centre
University of Worcester
Henwick Grove
WORCESTER
WR2 6AJ
UNITED KINGDOM

Share the world in peace and freedom.
The Earth and its people have no owners.

Isol – Argentina

one day, it will
be better.
Stay strong.

You are
welcome.

Maral Sassouni

MIGRATIONS exhibition
c/o Taz Lovejoy
DIGITAL ARTS CENTRE
UNIVERSITY of WORCESTER
HENWICK GROVE
WORCESTER WR2 6AJ
UNITED KINGDOM

One day it will be better.
Stay strong.
You are welcome.

Maral Sassouni – USA

I came to UK as a refugee in 1993 because of the war in
my country.... In my suitcase I had eleven paintbrushes.
I thought they would help me to survive in my new life.
Now I am a glass artist, have my safe nest (studio)
and am making little birds out of melted glass.

97   Maja Stanic – Bosnia & Herzegovina/UK

"Wherever you go
becomes
a part of you
somehow"
- Anita Desai

From: Renate Rogina
Latvia

To:
MIGRATIONS
exhibition
(ICPBS illustration)
Digital Arts Centre
University of Worcester
Henwick Grove
Worcester
WR2 6AF
United Kingdom

R LATVIJAS PASTS
RR 543769735 LV

Wherever you go becomes
a part of you somehow.

Anita Desai

Renate Logina – Latvia

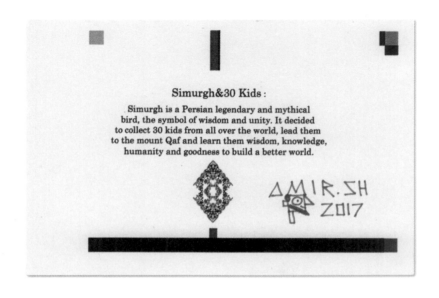

Simurgh is a Persian legendary and mythical bird, the symbol of wisdom and unity. It decided to collect 30 kids from all over the world, lead them to the mount Qaf and learn them wisdom, knowledge, humanity and goodness to build a better world.

Amir Shabanipour – Iran

We hope peace.

Mogu Takahashi – Japan

"Hope" is the thing with feathers –
That perches in the soul –
And sings the tune without
    the words –
And never stops – at all –

And sweetest – in the Gale –
    is heard –
And sore must be the storm –
That could abash the little Bird
That kept so many warm –

I've heard it in the chillest land –
And on the strangest Sea –
Yet – never – in Extremity,
It asked a crumb – of me.

Emily Dickinson

105   Jane Ray – UK

LEILA AJIRI, originally from Iran, now lives in Kreis Bergstrasse, Germany, where she is a professional artist and a prominent participant in promoting the integration of migrants in the community.

HELENA BERGENDAHL was born in Gothenburg, Sweden. Helena has illustrated many books for children and has served on the international jury for the Bratislava Illustration Biennale.

ALIDA BOTHMA lives in Greyton, South Africa. Among her international awards are a Merit and a Bronze from the UNESCO Noma Concours in Tokyo.

ALESSANDRA CIMATORIBUS was born in Friuli, Italy. Her books have been translated into 16 languages, and awards include the 2016 Top Exhibit Award for her murals at Philadelphia Zoo.

KATERINA DUBOVIK is an illustrator and designer, born in Minsk, Belarus, and now living in Amsterdam.

BRIAN FITZER is the pen-name of Brian Fitzgerald. He lives in Dublin, Ireland. His wordless *Bounce Bounce* won the international 'Silent Book' Award in 2014.

CHRISTOPHER CORR is a Londoner, who studied at the Royal College of Art, and still lives in the city. But a love of travel inspires his work, which, as he says, "is all about joy, colour and a love of life."

ANDY ROBERT DAVIES studied illustration at Loughborough University, UK. He is an illustration lecturer and professional illustrator both for children's and adult books and magazines, living in Malvern, Worcestershire.

NICOLA DAVIES has written many books for children about nature and wildlife, as well as being an accomplished artist in her own right. She was named Writer in Residence for 2018-19 at Book Trust UK.

JUDITH DREWS is published in more than 17 countries, and from 2008-15 was a member of the nominating body for the Astrid Lindgren Memorial Award. She lives in Berlin, Germany.

KSENIA EFIMOVA writes: "I am a mostly self-taught artist. Currently I am studying at a School of Digital Art in Saint Petersburg, upgrading my skills. I am also working as a freelance illustrator."

MOHAMMAD BARRANGI FASHTAMI writes: "I am both an artist and an athlete. I have a disability in my left hand, though I believe it is by no means a stymying limitation. Born in Rasht, a northern city in Iran, I love printmaking. I make them with my hand and using my leg."

GABRIELA GERMAIN FONCK studied drawing and design at Valparaiso Catholic University, Chile, and is a freelance illustrator and author. Her most recent book is *Cuando el Viento Sopla Fuerte*.

STEPHEN FOWLER specialises in rubber stamping and alternative printmaking. He grew up in Cornwall, graduated at Central St Martin's School of Art in London, and is Lecturer in Illustration at Worcester University's Institute of the Arts.

MARIE-LOUISE GAY was born in Québec City, Canada. Her work as an author and illustrator has earned many distinctions, including the Governor General's Award, the E.B. White Award, and the IBBY International Honor List.

INGA GRIMM was born in 1969 in Tübingen, Germany and has lived in Sweden since 1998. A self-taught artist, she creates colourful assemblages as well as graphic works.

DIEK GROBLER likes to depict "little disasters and small miracles". Born in South Africa, he has been exhibiting his work since 1988 in a range extending from fine art to animation.

PIET GROBLER is an award-winning South African illustrator and a graduate in Theology, Journalism and Visual Arts (Illustration). After nine years' lecturing in the UK, he returned to South Africa to be a freelance illustrator again. He is visiting professor in Illustration at the University of Worcester, UK.

NATALIA GUROVICH, a graduate graphic designer from the Universidad Católica de Chile, is currently a freelance illustrator in Mexico City. She has received numerous international awards and recognitions and to date has published more than 20 books.

RHIAN WYN HARRISON lives in South Devon, UK; she was a typographer and graphic designer and is now "a born again artist" specialising in mixed media illustration.

TOBIAS HICKEY is Course Leader in Illustration at the University of Worcester, UK. He studied graphic design at Liverpool Polytechnic and illustration at St Martin's School of Art, and his images are often seen in newspapers and magazines as well as in children's books. With Piet Grobler he is a founder of ICPBS.

STIAN HOLE is one of Norway's leading graphic designers and illustrators of children's books. His *Garmann's Summer* won an Ezra Jack Keats New Writer Award and Germany's Children's Literature Award in 2009. He lives in Oslo.

PETR HORÁČEK was born in Prague. He now lives in the UK. Since the Books for Children Newcomer Award in 2001, he has won many others, including the Royal Society Young People's Book Prize 2017 for *A First Book of Animals*.

MIES VAN HOUT was born in Eindhoven, Netherlands, and has been illustrating children's books for around 30 years. *Vrolijk* won a Vlag en Wimpel award in 2014.

ISOL is the pen-name of Marisol Misenta. Her contributions to international children's literature have gained her a Golden Apple Award in 2003 and the Astrid Lindgren Memorial Award in 2013. She lives in Buenos Aires.

RICHARD JOHNSON has illustrated more than fifty children's books in the past eighteen years, and has received Gold and Silver Awards for his work from the Association of Illustrators. *Once Upon a Snowstorm* was shortlisted for the World Illustration Awards in 2018. He lives in Lincolnshire, UK.

JON KLASSEN has won both the American Caldecott Medal and the British Kate Greenaway Medal for children's book illustration. Born in Winnipeg, Canada, he currently lives in Los Angeles, USA.

MYUNGAE LEE studied oriental painting at university. Her first book written and illustrated by herself, *Plastic Island* (2015) gained international honours at the Bologna International Children's Book Fair, the Nami Island International Picture Book Concours, and the BIB (Biennial of Illustrations Bratislava).

MARIA LEON is a Spanish nature artist who describes herself as "an enthusiastic biologist who likes to observe nature and paint around that". Born in A Coruña, she lives in Tarifa, Andalucia.

NEAL LAYTON was born in Chichester, UK, and now lives in Portsmouth. His *The Story of Stars* was the SLA Information Book prizewinner for 2014.

RENATE LOGINA lives in Riga, Latvia and is a graduate of the Art Academy of Latvia. A freelance illustrator, she is an expert in the games field as well as in traditional media.

P. J. LYNCH is a winner of the Mother Goose Award and Kate Greenaway Medal (twice). He was Ireland's Laureate na n'Óg in 2016, and lives in Dublin.

ROBERT MACFARLANE is a Fellow of Emmanuel College, Cambridge. His books on mountains, landscapes and travel have won many awards and have been published in more than twenty countries. With Jackie Morris, he is author of *The Lost Words: A Spell-Book.*

ROGER MELLO has illustrated over 100 books, and written 22. He has won many international prizes and awards including the 2014 Hans Christian Andersen Illustration Award. Born in Brasilia, he now lives in Rio de Janeiro.

JACKIE MORRIS has written and illustrated many books. Her sensitivity to the natural world shines in her work and led to her illustrations to *The Lost Words* being chosen by British booksellers as the most beautiful book of 2017. She lives in Pembrokeshire, Wales.

KANA OKITA is a freelance artist and graphic designer, a graduate of Musashino Art University, living in Tokyo.

PATRICIA GONZALEZ PALACIOS has been exhibiting her work in her homeland of Chile and in Spain since 1982. She is both an independent artist and a teacher of illustration.

BECKY PALMER graduated from the Cambridge School of Art in 2012. Her first graphic novel was published in France in 2014. Most recently, she illustrated *Ellie and Lump's Busy Day* by Dorothy Clarke, *Love Reading*'s Book of the Month for June 2017. She teaches children's book illustration at Anglia Ruskin University.

MARCELO PIMENTEL is one of Brazil's leading illustrators, born in Rio de Janeiro. His wordless book *O Fim da Fila (The End of the Line)* won the Grand Prix at the Nami Island Concours in 2015.

MARIJA PRELOG gained her diploma at the Academy of Graphic Arts in Ljubljana, Slovenia, and though she still lives in the city, she says that nature is her great source of inspiration for her many picture books and other works.

JANE RAY was born in London and studied art and design at Middlesex University. Since 1989 she has illustrated over 50 books and written several. Winner of a Smarties Award in 1992, she has six times been shortlisted for the Kate Greenaway Medal.

CHRIS RIDDELL is both a leading children's illustrator and writer and an acclaimed political cartoonist. Among his many awards are a UNESCO Prize for Children's Literature and three Kate Greenaway Medals. In 2015-17 he was UK Children's Laureate. He lives in Brighton, UK.

ROMB-BOM.COM is a Lithuanian online gallery of textile designs and artefacts, using historic and natural Baltic motifs, run by Gabrielius Mackevicius.

MARAL SASSOUNI grew up in Playa del Rey, California, and studied design and animation at UCLA. Since 1999 she has been based primarily in Paris. Her first book, *The Green Umbrella*, was a Bank Street Best Children's Book of the Year in 2017.

AXEL SCHEFFLER was born in Hamburg, Germany, and now lives in London. Since 1988 he has illustrated some of the world's best-loved children's books, including Julia Donaldson's *The Gruffalo*, which won the Smarties Prize in 1999. Their latest is *The Ugly Five* (2017).

AMIR SHABANIPOUR is a painter and illustrator, living in Rasht, Iran. He was a Selected Artist for the Illustrarte Award 2016, and his work has been exhibited at the Bologna Children's Book Fair.

CATARINA SOBRAL was born in Coimbra, Portugal and now lives in Lisbon. A writer as well as an illustrator, she won the Bologna Children's Book Fair International Award for Illustration in 2014.

MAYA STANIC grew up in Bosnia-Herzegovina and has a master's degree in product design from Sarajevo University. Now based in London, her fine work in stained glass can be seen in many locations.

MOGU TAKAHASHI lives and works in Tokyo. Since 2006 his work has been exhibited and published in many countries.

SHAUN TAN grew up in Perth, Western Australia, and has gained worldwide acclaim as an illustrator and film-maker. In 2011 he received the Astrid Lindgren Memorial Award for his contribution to international children's literature.

NELLEKE VERHOEFF lives in Rotterdam, Holland. She began as a performer but found her true vocation in art and illustration. *Concerto* was a finalist in the 2018 Silent Book Competition.

SATOKO WATANABE was born in Kyoto, Japan and studied oil painting and printing at Kyoto Seika University. He lives in Saitama, Japan.

MIRA WIDHAYATI is a graduate in Visual Communication Design at Bandung Institute of Technology, Indonesia, and is a member of Kelompok Pencinta Bacaan, the Society for the Advancement of Children's Literature.

YUVAL ZOMMER is a graduate of the Royal College of Art, London, and renowned for children's books that put the living world at the heart of storytelling. His *Big Book of Beasts* won the English Association 4-11 Book Award in 2018.

ACKNOWLEDGEMENTS

Grateful thanks are due to all the artists who contributed their works, also to IBBY for its support, and to Amnesty International for its endorsement. Also to Robert Bly for permission to use his translation of *Det er den Draumen*, and to Miranda Otter-Barry Ross for translations from Spanish.
The text of Emily Dickinson's 'Hope' is from *The Poems of Emily Dickinson*, edited by Thomas H. Johnson, The Belknap Press of Harvard University Press.
Every effort has been made to trace copyright holders of texts quoted from. If any copyright items have been inadvertently included, the publishers will be glad to be informed and to make acknowledgement in any future edition.

All royalties from this book will be donated to Amnesty International and IBBY.

Peregrine is pilgrim-bird – world-wanderer, cloud-splitter

Ever looked up, seen peregrine

Race sun across the sky, leave light for dust?

Ever wondered what it must be like to

Ghost over borders, as peregrine does?

Rise from ground now, up by quick wing-flicks and gyre

Into air, where frontiers fade fast.

Never stop dreaming of flying further, higher,

Ending up where the heart hopes for, longs for, at last.

Robert Macfarlane and Jackie Morris, UK